BÔ YIN RÂ
(JOSEPH ANTON SCHNEIDERFRANKEN)

THE GATED GARDEN
VOLUME 11

THE WISDOM
OF ST. JOHN

SECOND, REVISED EDITION

For more information
about the books of Bô Yin Râ and
titles available in English translation,
visit the Kober Press web site at
www.kober.com.

THE KOBER PRESS PUBLISHES THE ONLY ENGLISH TRANSLATIONS
OF THE BOOKS OF BÔ YIN RÂ AUTHORIZED BY THE KOBER VERLAG,
SWITZERLAND. THE KOBER VERLAG PUBLISHES THE BOOKS OF
BÔ YIN RÂ IN THE ORIGINAL GERMAN AND HAS PROTECTED
THEIR INTEGRITY SINCE THE AUTHOR'S LIFETIME.

BÔ YIN RÂ
(JOSEPH ANTON SCHNEIDERFRANKEN)

THE WISDOM OF ST. JOHN

TRANSLATED FROM THE GERMAN
BY B.A. REICHENBACH

BERKELEY, CALIFORNIA

English translation copyright © 1975 by B. A. Reichenbach
Second, revised edition English translation ©2016
by B. A. Reichenbach

Eric W. Strauss, Publisher & Editor

All rights reserved.

For permission to quote or excerpt, contact The Kober Press
Email: koberpress@mindspring.com

This book is an authorized translation from the German of
Bô Yin Râ's *Die Weisheit des Johannes*, copyright 1924 by
Kober'sche Verlagsbuchhandlung, Basel-Leipzig (now Kober
Verlag AG, Bern, Switzerland (www.koberverlag.ch)).

Printed in the United States of America

Library of Congress Catalog Card Number: 74-15272

International Standard Book Number: 978-0-915034-28-4

Typography and composition by Dickie Magidoff

Book cover after a design by Bô Yin Râ

CONTENTS

   Introduction 7
1 The Master's Image 23
2 The Luminary's Mortal Life 33
3 The Aftermath 55
4 The Missive 69
5 The Authentic Teaching 81
6 The Paraclete 105
   Conclusion 117

TO
FRAU HELENE SCHNEIDERFRANKEN
AND HER DAUGHTERS

INTRODUCTION

From all this follows that I commend to you again and again the Gospel of John, for in it you have all of Moses and the prophets, of the evangelists and the apostles.
>   Goethe writing to Herder
>   20 February 1786

HIDDEN RIVERS SEND THEIR TOLLING WAVES in solemn echoes through the ages, and all the noises of the day can never drown that timeless sound for those who care to hear it.

The many who are causing so much noise have long grown nearly deaf, and now can only hear the shrillest blare before their very ears. Yet in every age one also can find others: souls who shun the noisy carnivals, but in the quiet of the night will listen for the solemn, distant echoes rising from the heart of never-ending Life.

However, there are times when those who listen are becoming many, and when their senses grow so keen that even through the deafening thunder by which the world around them seems benumbed, they hear the sacred echoes of eternity more clearly than all the noises that would hinder them.

WE NOW LIVE at the dawn of such an age.

Every day finds more and more of those who hear.

And they no longer will pay heed to raucous mountebanks, nor to the roar of captured lions; they shall not hear the castanets of frenzied dancers, and with a smile they will ignore the bells that tinkle from the motley caps of fools.

They, instead, will only listen for the solemn echoes from the shores of all eternity; and near and far, in time and place, they will be seeking their own kind: others who can testify that also they perceive these timeless echoes everywhere.

INTRODUCTION

The best today are weary of all the "wisdom" that is nothing more than *intellect*.

Feats of acrobatic thinking have long appealed to none but aged children, or the childish old.

The subtle speculations of overweening sophists today are little more than token coinage even to the always simpleminded herd, and nowadays one seldom gains its favor with such currency, as sailors once could buy the good will of the natives with colored beads and strings of glassy pearls.

But one who is not far from his awakening, and would give value to his life in purposeful, intelligent activity, he will require knowledge of a different kind. What he shall need is knowledge of absolute and lasting certainty: knowledge that will not—perhaps tomorrow—once more become *uncertainty*, because its very fundaments at any moment may be undermined again by someone else's probing mind.

In every age in history there were a few who had attained such final certainty.

It is not found through logic or philosophy, and never can the human mind create it out of thoughts.

It is not wealth of learning one needs in order to receive it.

Whoever you may be, however highly others might esteem your knowledge: you never will know final certainty until you learn to lay aside the glittering kaleidoscope of intellectual speculation.

Through the workings of your mind you have produced a labyrinth, and in its vicious circles you have lost your way.

You cannot find yourself again unless you will retrace your steps, back to the entrance of this maze, back to the point where once your thinking was *uncomplicated*, like the thinking of a child.

Even at the dawn of time one never came to final knowledge any other way.

The cosmic Light to which the ancient sages have borne witness—testimony that today one reads with awe—shines in timeless radiance even at this very day; but if you seek it in the gloomy tunnels of your mind you may indeed deny that such a Light exists—for into this domain it does not send its rays.

THE ANCIENTS often had far more "dominion of the earth" than all the later generations who, by idle fantasies and speculations, kept proudly raising ever higher the very walls which then imprisoned man's horizon of eternity.

The ancients, guided by enlightened insight, were able to sift truth from error, and thus would always with due reverence take over from their forebears what these bequeathed to them of their eternal wisdom. Thus, out of the ruins of all older temples they always rescued what was sacred. And even if in every later sanctuary a new and different image was enshrined, it did remain a veil and symbol for the selfsame godhead, and it was known as such to all who were informed.

The generations of the now declining age, however, who were themselves more deeply steeped in superstitions than they dreamed, although they haughtily proclaimed their fancies and hypotheses as "knowledge"—they would only see the "idol" in every sacred image of the past, and in the idol's cult saw nothing but the ancients' "superstition." They did not notice that behind each sacred cult there also stands profoundest wisdom; only this is hidden to the spiritually immature.

❧

AND SO THE ancient Missive, which now is called the Gospel according to St. John, was looked upon by many not so long ago—and perhaps still is by many even now—as little more than a mere fairy tale: a story full of poetry-inspired passages of long ago outmoded superstition.

Having overcome at last the ancient fear of critically looking at the temporal and human traces in the word of Holy Writ—long believed to have been written by the Holy Ghost—one had discovered marks of older heathen doctrines in that Missive's text. And as one further noticed that the lofty image of the godlike man presented in this old account bore traits of sundry older deities, it came about that many moderns—excepting the professing Christians—considered the entire text as little more than pious fabrication.

This view was not a little strengthened by the form in which the ancient text is known today; for this shows all too clearly that in its present state it merely is the last result of more than one redactor's unenlightened labor.

Nor did it much improve the text that from the very first one sought to represent it as a work of the disciple whom the Master "loved," and therefore spared no effort to make it match the other, older sources that bore legendary witness to the Master's earthly life: interweaving truth and fiction at the pleasure of their authors.

And so one later could no longer recognize that the author of this ancient text—first written more than a lifetime after the Master's death—had merely *used* the older works that tell about his earthly life, but that his own intent was very different from the desire of only adding yet another book of wonder-lore to those already in existence.

Here it will be necessary to explain that in reality this ancient Missive, which its first redactors had ascribed to John—the pupil whom the Master "loved"—was written by another, but one who had found timeless knowledge; however, what he wrote was meant for *his* disciples, who long had known by word of mouth the essence of a sacred teaching that truly came as "tidings of great joy" to all who heard of it—and understood.

I also speak from certain knowledge if I say here that the author of the Missive still possessed old manuscripts that contained in faithful copy parts of letters personally written by the Master. After the latter's death, John had taken custody of the originals, and later on had let his own disciples copy them.

It further must be stated in this context that the disciple whom the Master "loved" was in fact the only one among the twelve "apostles" who knew the final secrets connected with his Master's mission.

Following the Master's death, John gathered around himself the few who from the first had spiritually grasped the Master's teaching.

When John himself had died, the little flock of his disciples stayed together, and guarded as their own most secret knowledge facts that never could be reconciled with the beliefs and dogmas of the public cult, which soon had formed as a result of what the other pupils taught. From them, however, John had, soon after the Master's death, begun withdrawing more and more, even though the legend—which the cult created for itself—is striving to present him as one still very close to them.

The pupils following John's own disciples were the readers for whom the author wrote the text that I shall have to speak of in these pages. John's successors should not, however, be confused with the disciples of the Baptist, who also bore the name "Jehohanan."

John's pupils could truly not be taken in by tales of wondrous miracles, as they today appear in the corrupted text that was transmitted to posterity; even though, for later generations, certain of these legends may lend more profile to the Master's temporal appearance.

The miracle of which John's pupils knew, instead, was one within the Spirit; it was a miracle compared to which all signs and wonders of the legends paled—and such a miracle they knew from personal *experience*.

But while they carefully preserved, as their most sacred heritage, the radiant Master's teaching, as John had once received it, they also did not hesitate, wherever in the teachings of their day they found the threads of hidden truth, to weave such elements as well into the temple curtain that, in their sanctuaries, protected secrets from the eyes of the profane.

Only if all this is duly borne in mind can one—even now—perceive the genuine fragments of the author's text: by means of their inherent worth; and this despite the many hands that once had tampered with his manuscript, and in those parts at least that had escaped the narrow-minded censors of the early days.

But in the light of this, one will appreciate why Goethe ranked this text above all other books of Scripture; in striking contrast to more recent scholarship, which had to muster all its ingenuity that it might find at least one halfway passable approach to clear away the overgrowth that now has all but swallowed up this former garden of enlightened wisdom, whose order learned research is expected to restore.

༄

INTRODUCTION

AND IF THE reader now should wonder upon what kind of knowledge the present writer might have drawn that he is able to aver, for this and every future age, what he is bound to publish in this book, this writer first would have to dispel the assumption that what is stated here might be results of his "research."

The paths that lead to certain knowledge in questions of this kind are very steep and narrow, and all one's personal belongings—even the sublimest insights of the intellect—must be left behind, lest the climber's step should falter as he scales these awesome heights.

Indeed, there *is* a way of knowing whereby one can gain certainty in matters such as these; nor is there any other way to reach this certain knowledge.

But "proof" is known here only to the few who have themselves, since ages immemorial, preserved this way of knowing; and who, in every generation, pass on to others—proven like themselves—what they in turn had once received in this same way: the faculty of knowing by virtue of *self-transformation*, whereby the knower comes to knowledge through the very object of his knowing.

Such, however, is the knowledge on which this book is based.

※

I WISH TO offer certainty, and know that certainty cannot be found in any other way.

It is not my intention to persuade the reader to "believe" what I am saying.

Whoever would discover for himself if what I say is true, let him seek confirmation in himself: within his inmost self.

The reader shall not lose his time if he will learn to see what I must show him; and to see it in the way I have to show it.

※

AT TIMES IT may appear that I have strayed too far beyond the topic of this book, and one will also find some repetitions. I do not feel obliged, however, to write according to the rules of fiction.

Nor should this book be taken as a commentary on the work ascribed to the apostle John.

The present work has but a single aim: to show again the Master's authentic teaching; teachings that the writer of the ancient text could presuppose as something known among his readers.

And then I also would correct the age-old error that takes this Missive as a document inspired by the same beliefs as the three older records about the life of the "Anointed One," to which accounts, however, it very soon became attached—after it had been sufficiently re-edited.

It also will be necessary to place more emphasis on certain sayings in the ancient text, which were not only meant as incidental points of explanation or example; for then they also could have passed in their accepted sense.

M<small>AY THEN</small> the timeless wisdom that to this day shines brightly through the pages of this ancient text—despite all later efforts to obscure it—may this work, which now is called the "Gospel according to St. John," once more become a guiding star to all who seek: a guiding star to light their way into the Spirit.

CHAPTER ONE

THE MASTER'S IMAGE

To those who were professing their faith in his name, he had become a "God." To others, who had never understood the real meaning of his teaching, he seemed a victim of unearthly dreams. To later times, however, the radiant Master who brought "glad tidings" to the world has been transmitted in an image that only in the barest outline still retains some faint resemblance to his real likeness here on earth.

And yet, if anyone would truly understand the Master's timeless teaching, he first of all must gain a clear conception of the temporal and human likeness of the sublime "Anointed One"—lest he fall prey to idle fantasies and charm himself with languid, pious dreams.

༄

The RECORDS present him saying:

> WHY DO YOU CALL ME GOOD? NO ONE IS GOOD BUT GOD ALONE!

And truly, he would have been infuriated if one of those about him had ever dared to show him honors that were due to the Divine, or to address him as a "God."

And in the same way that he once had chased the money-changers and the merchants from the Temple of their God, so would he—with a "whip of cords"—have driven from his sight the first who might have dared to tell him: "Master, the time will come when also you shall have your temples!"

To be sure, he knew full well of his exalted station in the world of Spirit, no matter how at times he felt afraid and little.

Yet where on earth could any man be found who never showed himself but in the perfect knowledge of his highest worth and strength?

At times when all his consciousness is radiant in spiritual union with the "Father," whom the Eternal Word reveals out of Eternal Light—

the "Ancient of Days" who is in the "Beginning": Man Eternal in his original creation —then his word grows powerful and he feels raised above all fetters of this world.

Here then the Luminary, the Bearer of Eternal Light, reveals himself in the abundance of his power in the Spirit.

Yet, when at other times he feels the bonds of mortal life, he also does not hide the deepest anguish of his soul, and then it seems as if his timeless wisdom threatened to desert him.

> NOW MY SOUL IS TROUBLED. WHAT SHALL I SAY? FATHER, SAVE ME FROM THIS HOUR!

He never stands aloof from human company, even where the people are clearly not his followers, but is always cheerful with the joyous, and sad with those who mourn.

Compassion makes him the protector of the poor and the oppressed, the class to which he too belongs; yet at the same time he makes friends with wealthy and distinguished men.

He does not turn his back on hospitality, even where he knows his hosts are skeptical about his mission, and only had invited him to meet so singular a guest.

Wherever he finds kindness in a human soul, he too shows deepest love and understanding; only hypocrites and hearts of stone will make him utter scathing words.

He does not force his teaching on the world, but where he feels that people seek it, although it was not known to them as such, he tells them what he thinks they surely ought to understand.

He is not seeking honors, but where men honor him he feels that he is truly worthy to be honored. And when on one occasion a narrow mind among his followers complains of waste because a precious ointment has been used to refresh the Master's feet, instead of being sold to help the poor, he calmly remarks:

> THE POOR YOU ALWAYS HAVE WITH YOU, BUT ME YOU HAVE NOT ALWAYS.

And here he did not mean—as later exegesis was to claim—that he "foresaw" his nearing end, but merely that he seldom came to visit the same town.

Nothing in man's nature was unknown to him, and well he knew of the relentless struggle between man's spiritual nature and the not easily controlled desires of the mortal creature.

> YOU CONDEMN ACCORDING TO APPEARANCE, BUT I CONDEMN NO ONE, FOR ALSO THE FATHER CONDEMNS NO ONE.

Radiant in the knowledge of his mission, he declares one might destroy this "Temple"—the ruling doctrine of the priests—and in "three days" he dared to "raise it up" again.

Those who heard him say these words knew very well of what he spoke, but they took careful note of it, so that they later might accuse him of "blasphemy" against the Temple.

But sometimes he does not greatly mind if people fail to understand him, when he must see that no amount of explanation would bring about the comprehension that he seeks.

In the fullest knowledge of his spiritually singular position among the generations of his time, he can declare majestically:

YOU ARE FROM BENEATH, I AM FROM ABOVE.

YOU ARE OF THIS WORLD, I AM NOT OF THIS WORLD.

But unlike those about him, he also knew the source to which he owed his timeless dignity; knew of the many years of spiritual discipline, and of the bitter struggle in himself through which he in the end had found that absolute authority from which he then could speak and teach "not as the scribes."

His mission's deepest mystery was known to very few, and even those had failed to understand it, except for the disciple whom he "loved."

He alone among the pupils knew also of his Master's spiritual origins, and of the final causes of his right to teach.

When following the Master's death the "flock was scattered," this pupil gathered those who were his spiritual kind, and then revealed his deeper knowledge to all who proved themselves as worthy of his guidance.

The little circle of the spiritually guided and enlightened that had formed around John was not to disappear until much later, when long the public cult had grown in strength and number: a cult that grew out of existing ancient rites, and then transformed the Master's human likeness into the Godhead of its worship.

Condemned as "heretics," John's pupils passed into obscurity, and with them vanished the authentic image of the Master, who never in his life had claimed that he was the "Messiah," and who, indeed, would have considered it a desecration of his words to base himself on sayings of the ancient prophets, which must be seen in a quite different light, but wherein other minds—when he himself had long been dead—would fancy that he was "foretold."

CHAPTER TWO

THE LUMINARY'S MORTAL LIFE

It here is made my task and duty to describe the Master's spiritual unfolding. Historians of his time took little note of his existence, but owing to the tales and legends growing up around his life, and also through a cult that used his name to give new life to ancient mystic rites, he became a great enigma, fraught with contradictions, and has remained so to this day.

I shall relate what can be known by those who have their knowledge from experience, and thus can speak with certainty on what has long since passed from outward observation.

He was born in Nazareth in Galilee, and thus was called a "Nazarene"—not, as some suppose, after a sect of mystics. He was still a little child when his father took him, together with his mother, into Egypt, where at that time the father's craft was in demand and well rewarded. From this, which did in fact occur, would later grow the legendary "Flight into Egypt."

A few years later he was back in his native city; and now, as soon as he was old enough, he started helping at his father's work. And so he learned, at first almost in play, to do some simple chores and duties, as these seemed fitting for his age and strength.

Thus, quite early in his youth, he had become a fellow craftsman to his father. To be a carpenter in those days meant, however, that he not only learned how wood was used for building and construction, but also how to make some of the sturdier tools that people used in house and field.

To acquire even the most basic elements of erudition, he neither had the time, nor was it then the custom that a youthful craftsman without means should have the like ambition.

His spiritual development, which I shall presently discuss, had been completed long before he learned the art of writing in the letters of his native tongue; in this he was instructed by some learned men whose friendship he had won by then.

Here then is the background of his spiritual unfolding.

From his father he had only heard the customary prayers that by tradition every pious Jew was wont to say.

Every Sabbath he would hear the usual interpretation of the Law, handed down from ancient times.

But since he could not read the sacred books himself, his knowledge here again was very much restricted.

However, even from his early youth, when tired from his labor, although still fresh in spirit, he would be resting on his humble bed, he knew a wondrous kind of inner guidance. He kept this very secret, even from his parents, but did believe that through this spiritual experience he more and more could understand the wisdom in the Law: like those

—he thought—who had the learning needed to consult the Scriptures.

Yet from time to time he gave himself away, when on the Sabbath or on holy days he heard the elders of the congregation speak on questions of the Law, and then was able, through his inner guidance, to give a fitting answer. And thus the later legend, which shows him teaching as a boy among the learned elders in the Temple of the Holy City, is in substance based on fact; even though the doctors at Jerusalem were doubtless not the first to marvel at his wisdom.

At Capernaum, in his later adolescence, he had his first encounter with a Luminary, one of the Bearers of Eternal Light, whose exalted Brother he was destined to become, since by kind he had been one of them long before he saw the sunlight of this world. He then was working at Capernaum for several weeks on a commission from his father, with whose kinsmen he was lodging.

However, on that first occasion he did not know whom he had really met that peaceful evening hour by the lake; a man he now saw very often at that place: one who had the power to open more and more his heart, and made him see the inmost mysteries of Being.

But soon there followed more encounters of this kind, so that he finally no longer even thought it strange that he should be receiving such profound enlightenment through men who evidently were connected in some way. However, all of this he kept a secret, for so he was instructed.

When in this way he had continued for some years, his inner knowledge ever growing, one of these men—whom now he knew as old and trusted friends, although he bowed in awe before them—came to him one day and told him: that now the time had come that he begin a regular, more systematic kind of schooling, but that this would not interfere with the performance of his daily work.

It was to be the purpose of this schooling, he was told, to make him capable of comprehending the deepest wisdom of the Law, and not alone to know it for himself, but also that he might reveal this light to others: so that the many who sought nurture for their soul in Holy Writ be given more than the unprofitable commentaries of the scribes, which were like stones when handed to the hungry begging for bread.

From that day on he consciously received the inner spiritual guidance of those who were his kind.

His daily work did not prevent him from going through this schooling, nor from passing every trial it required.

Whenever he would falter, or fears and doubts began to threaten him, one of his teachers would quietly come to his side: to strengthen him in faith, and to dispel the demon world that was about to frighten him.

AFTER YEARS of strictest discipline, he one day had attained his full maturity; and now that all the scales had fallen from his eyes, he could at last behold himself in his exalted mission.

The night was radiant with stars when, on a rocky mountain height not far from his abode, he did receive his final consecration as a Bearer of Eternal Light, as a Master of Knowledge and Love: as a Luminary among Luminaries.

Now he *knew* he was the Way, the Truth, and Life born within the Sun of Suns, out of the Light that shines through the Eternities.

※

From this day on he also spoke in public about his knowledge and experience, and clearly told others what he had received.

Now he spoke with fullest knowledge of his own authority, and on the basis of the sacred books, which now were open to him from within, he sought to show the deepest meaning in the ancient seers' words; yet at the same time he still carried on his work as he had done before.

But those who heard him speak were quite astonished at his words, and could not understand where he, a carpenter without formal learning, might all at once have gained such extraordinary insights.

Indeed, the transformation of his nature struck all his friends and relatives as something so unheard of that, disregarding the great wisdom of his words, they thought he had gone "mad"; and finally he could no longer live within his native city.

THE WISDOM OF ST. JOHN

And so he left his home, looking for some other place to settle, where people did not know him; there he hoped to earn his living with his work, and to awaken men's souls with his words.

But no matter where he turned, he found no town where he could stay; for he said things no man had ever said before, and many of the learned scribes were jealous because the people seemed to put more faith in him than in the doctrines they were teaching. For some time then he moved from town to town, until he once again turned to Capernaum, of which he had grown fond; for here he once had met the first of his eternal Brothers, who also now assured him that in this city he would find at last the rest for which he longed.

Here then, at Capernaum, he won the friendship of a wealthy man who joyfully received him in his house and listened to his words with fervent admiration. In this man's house he also met some learned friends, who taught him, in that sheltered haven, to read and write the letters of his native tongue.

୬

THE great esteem that he enjoyed here in the midst of highly honored men had soon begun to spread his fame abroad.

But as the people in those days believed that wise men of his kind were also given secret powers, and thus could heal all manner of diseases, there always came new patients to the house of his distinguished host, asking that the learned rabbi heal them.

At first the Master would not hear of such requests and sent the sick to the physicians.

But soon he was besieged by growing numbers, and from compassion he came out to comfort the afflicted. It happened, however, that many of those he had touched soon afterwards felt cured, so that at first he was not sure himself what he should make of these events.

Only now he could no longer disregard the pleas of the afflicted, who asked no more of him than that he merely touch them.

Even from afar they brought their sick before him, and all the time their faith in his apparent "wonder-working" powers grew. But whenever someone claimed that he was healed, the

Master stressed that nothing but the patient's faith had cured him.

He also strictly charged each patient not to spread the news of his recovery, for already he felt barely able to deal with their increasing numbers.

However, in the course of time he came to recognize that he indeed possessed a faculty for healing, and that the patients' faith was not the only cause of their recovery.

To be sure, he was not able to cure every patient, but even so the numbers he had healed kept rising day by day.

He had to spend long hours every day to lay his hands on all who came that he might cure them.

And far into the night he found himself surrounded by an audience that listened spellbound to his new interpretation of the Law. And here, among these listeners, he also found the first of those he felt were suited to become his closer pupils.

To them alone did he reveal the source from which he himself had once received his wisdom.

By now he long had realized that henceforth he could not continue working in his craft.

Yet as he knew that he would always find abundance for his daily needs if he, obedient to the Spirit's law, left it to his "Father" to feed and clothe him, his mind was free from care. And so he asked his host one day to grant him leave: that he might also teach in other places.

The enmity he had encountered in the past now seemed to him no longer any reason for concern.

His first disciples, whom he had chosen at Capernaum, refused to part with him, however, and so they followed where he went. Each of them would in his own way take to heart the wisdom that their Master had to give them.

In many places he was joyfully received, with his disciples, because he was a famous healer; but elsewhere he could also meet with rude rejection. Only for the townsmen of his native city he was never more than the presumptuous "madman" they had judged him from the first.

The common people, on the other hand, would call his healings—where they could occur—great "miracles," and did not understand him when he stressed in every case that such apparent miracles resulted only from the patient's faith, and from a given power flowing from the healer's body.

The ancient teachings of his nation he would interpret in a way that gave them meaning even in the sight of higher knowledge; only where he saw the souls oppressed by sterile ceremonialism, or where the gloomy tribal god of former times still claimed his sacrifices would he say:

> IT WAS SAID TO THEM OF FORMER DAYS ... BUT I SAY UNTO YOU ....

⚘

A<small>FTER HE</small> had moved from place to place in Galilee almost for a year, healing and teaching with varying success, he came to be convinced that only at Jerusalem could he expect to find the echo that he needed. His patrons at Capernaum already had announced him to their own friends in the Holy City, and, with the best of introductions, he and his disciples now joined the other pilgrims who journeyed to Jerusalem to celebrate the Passover.

His distinguished hosts received him with great hospitality, but already his first appearance in public earned him the hatred of the Temple's priesthood.

For this reason he soon left Jerusalem, but did not return to Galilee; instead, he stayed nearby and now and then still came into the city on shorter visits. But in the end he more and more avoided Jerusalem, as it became quite clear to him that even his distinguished friends would be unable to protect him if ever he should fall into the hands of the priesthood, for he had bitterly attacked them in his speeches.

W<small>HEREVER HE</small> stayed, he taught and healed as he had done in Galilee.

And thus it could not be prevented that he became a rising hope for ever wider circles of the population, especially among the poor and disenfranchised, who hated their despotic priesthood even more than the oppressors from abroad.

And so it came about that all the people in the land grew more and more convinced that he was finally the man their ancient books—as they believed—had promised: the One who now would have to free the country's poor, both from the Roman tyranny, and from the yoke they had to carry for their priests.

Those among the city's ever restless populace who were of this belief had learned that, shortly before the Passover, the Master would again be coming to Jerusalem. And so they made all preparations necessary to proclaim him as their king as soon as he arrived; for to their eyes the power of the priesthood was only guarded by the Roman cohorts, and in their blindness they had no conception of the might of Rome.

And as the Master now approached, they all went out to welcome him before the city gates in joyous exultation—men, women, and children—and their spokesmen came to him demanding that he lead them against their oppressors.

Overwhelmed by everything he saw, he briefly lost the sureness of his inner counsel; and as Moses in the legend once had doubted whether he could furnish water for the people, so he in turn believed, even though for moments only, that the power he was offered might become a basis for his mission.

Only too soon he realized his error, so that he scarcely had entered the city when he withdrew from the excited multitude and sought shelter in the house of one of his distinguished friends, until the crowds had been dispersed by soldiers of the Roman garrison.

But the consequences of his fleeting error could now no longer be escaped, neither on the spiritual nor on the temporal plane.

The priests of the Temple had long felt hatred for him as a scathing censor; besides, they feared his growing influence among the people. And now he had himself provided the ideal pretext for charging him before the Roman government: as one who rioted against the Roman rule, an agitator of the people who wanted to become their king.

※

To be sure, the Roman government had long been used to tumults in this nation, and would have much preferred to simply overlook this latest incident as well; however, in view of this specific charge, it was no longer possible to circumvent arresting the accused.

The Roman procurator, worldly-wise and skeptical, could clearly see that he was being used; and as he felt offended in his pride, he sought to extricate himself from having to pass sentence.

He therefore turned the trial over to those who had preferred the charges.

He little did suspect how much it pleased the latter that now they could condemn the hated censor according to their native law as well, and, seemingly, on strictly valid grounds.

Indeed, he had said many things that earlier they had not dared to challenge, and these could now be used as pretexts to demand his death. Besides, he had "blasphemed" against the Temple—what more was needed! But since the Roman government did not permit that they put any man to death, they needed only to persist in charging that the man had led astray the people, and that he wanted to become their king, in order to compel the Roman jurisdiction to execute the hate-born sentence in their stead.

The outcome was: the man they hated died—perished on the gibbet of the Roman cross—after Roman mercenaries from every corner of the globe, and Jewish sergeants of the Temple, already had tortured him almost to death.

But only now, in this his dying hour, when all his work on earth appeared already ended, did the Master in effect accomplish his sublimest work of Love: a work of such immeasurable power, that all who see the worlds of the eternal Spirit will honor him throughout eternity as the most radiant among the Luminaries: the Lord of Love to all who ever knew of love on earth. And there can never come another who might approach the awesome greatness of the love that he embodied.

THE WISDOM OF ST. JOHN

For in his final hour he succeeded in wholly unifying in himself: the human mortal creature and the powers of the Spirit; and in this unified, eternal consciousness he found the strength to love the very men who were destroying him on earth; indeed, could love them—even as himself—and in the very hour of his agony.

The physically invisible dimension of this earth, which holds this globe surrounded as an egg contains its yolk, was freed for all eternity in this most sacred hour, and wrested from the powers of the "Prince of this world." This unseen, mighty Being, who is merely conscious of himself, but not within the Spirit, seeks only to experience his *own* reality; and, living in the loveless night of matter, would draw into his own experience all things that exist.

As he himself was vanquished in that final hour, so all the might of darkness can now be conquered on this earth: by those who know that man can gain this power, and who possess "good will"—whose will proceeds from love.

※

I<small>F MAN ON</small> earth were conscious of his power, he truly would have changed this planet's face in these almost two thousand years, so that the generations that now still have to bear the burdens of this life would find prepared for them a form of physical existence that to their eyes would seem to be "Elysium."

To be sure, man never can create a real "Garden of Eden" on this earth; but what he may indeed accomplish is so lofty that future generations shall truly once look back with horror upon the traces of man's present deeds; as we today may shudder when we unearth the graves of man's half-beast, half-human forebears, and find that they were feeding on the bones and marrow of their slaughtered foes, and sucked the brains out of their victims' skulls.

Not until man recognizes what works he can accomplish through the might of Love, and then will seek to change this present world—not until that time shall the sublimest work of Love, the work of Golgotha, bear lasting fruit for all humanity.

CHAPTER THREE

THE AFTERMATH

The greatest work that ever man on earth was able to accomplish was accomplished once on Golgotha: for in that death upon the cross the destiny of mortal man, of all humanity, has been set free from cosmic thraldom.

It now remains to give account of what took place after the Master had died, for here the zeal of pious fantasy has from the first concealed the facts: in order that the truth might be forever hidden from posterity.

To be sure, the sacred legend holds the core of truth, and those who can discover it behind its veil shall not lose their reward.

Thus, the Luminary, the Bearer of Eternal Light, had truly "risen" from his earthly grave;

but in this Resurrection no mortal form could any longer be a vessel for his Being.

Again, it is quite true that even to this day the Luminary has not left this earth; indeed, those of his spiritual Brothers who have their task on earth as mortals can see him in his *spiritual* likeness, which perfectly reflects his former physical appearance such as his pupils once had known it.

All this, however, does not mean that the historical realities connected with the Master's passing are of no consequence for later generations.

Therefore, let the facts be known: as they are known to those who see. The more so as the essence of the pious faith, which through the centuries gave joy and comfort to so many, nowadays no longer needs symbolic veils. On the contrary, the veils present the danger that the Faith's eternal substance will not be found by those who seek it.

Here now follows what in fact occurred.

THE AFTERMATH

As soon as the Master had died, his distinguished friends did all they could to get possession of his body through the Roman procurator, since all their efforts to avert the execution had been unsuccessful.

The governor, however, was more than willing now to grant them their request; given that he earlier had not been able, despite his best intentions, to spare the Master's life on their behalf. The procurator's sympathies had from the first been with the Master's friends, while for the priesthood of the Temple he felt only deep contempt, because they had been able to force him to sentence a man to death who, in his judgment, never was the slightest danger to the state.

But when the chief priests learned of this, and knew for certain that the procurator would not hear them, they instead besieged the prefect of the city garrison, and persuaded him to give them soldiers who should guard the grave; for they greatly feared that otherwise the dead man's followers might come to mourn their grief before the sepulcher, and then could turn their fury on the priests.

And so the tomb received a Roman guard, who were to see that no assemblies gathered at the site.

❧

However, at that time there still resided in seclusion, in the mountains of Judea, the Master's spiritual Brothers who once had taught and guided him, as one of their own kind, toward the perfection of his priestly kingship. In the days of his public ministry the Master had often met them in the wilderness, and many times had gone to visit their remote abodes.

They knew what had befallen him, but were unable to protect him: because his spiritual transgression—his fleeting impulse to ally himself with worldly power had forced his fate out of the hands of that high guidance in the Spirit to which they all were subject. He too had known this guidance: before he briefly let himself become deluded, on entering Jerusalem, by the impetuous demands of those who saw in him the temporal redeemer, come to free them from political oppression.

The transmutation of the laws that rule the unseen regions of this earth—the very work that he was to accomplish by his deed of Love on Golgotha—would have spared him what he had to suffer: if another had accomplished it before him.

But since this transmutation could not be brought about but in his final hour, and by him alone, his spiritual Brothers, deeply grieved and yet within their hearts rejoicing in expectation of his triumph, were forced to let him walk his way of sorrow.

Now, however, they knew about the Master's grave. He himself, indeed, was present in their midst in spiritual likeness.

Thus, they did what needed to be done—with his consent and by his will—that his remains might not become the object of some foolish cult.

Among them there was one who could induce a magic sleep in people by merely getting them to talk and answer questions.

This one alone now walked up to the soldiers at the grave; and since his garments were like those of Roman dignitaries, the guards respectfully replied to all his questions, until their tongues grew heavy and they at last sank to the ground, overcome by sleep and dreams.

It now was time to call the other Brothers, who had been waiting near the grave.

The tomb was opened with some difficulty, and with greatest care they then brought out the body. Still wrapped in its bandages for burial, they laid it on two lengths of cloth that they had brought. It was placed in such a way that one piece would support the lower, the other piece the upper body.

Without delay they carried their beloved, weighty burden through the moonlit night, and with much effort made their way far up into the mountains, to a rocky gorge that had been chosen earlier. Here, where on the day before they had prepared a pyre, two more among his Brothers were already waiting.

These Brothers, however, were distinguished men of foreign race who once had come from distant countries in the East. And following the custom of their land, the treasured body now was offered to the flames: at a place where they were safe from every interruption. The brightness of the moonlight also paled the fire's glow, and as for miles around no human dwelling could be found at that time in this desert region, a fire would not have attracted much attention, even if the gorge itself had not protected it from being seen within the wide terrain.

WHEN IN the light of early dawn the flames were dying down, his Brothers carefully collected everything that had remained, wrapped it up in sheets, and made their way on foot in one long journey toward the Jordan: to bury in the waters of this river the final traces of the Master's earthly life, as was the custom in their native land.

Having returned to their secluded mountain dwellings, they stayed there yet a certain time and now and then would visit those among the Master's pupils who spiritually were still close to him after he had left the visible world.

But twelve months later they took their leave of Palestine forever and once more traveled to the East: returning to their native lands, which lay not far from where the highest mountains rise on earth.

THE WISDOM OF ST. JOHN

൞

These brothers were in truth the legend's "wise men from the East"—the priestly kings and royal priests—who once had noticed "far off in the East" the "star" of the young carpenter from Galilee, and who had come to teach and guide him until the day when he himself could comprehend his mission. They had not come, however, to kneel before the infant's cradle with their presents, as they would later be presented in the legend.

The legend rather formed—in its own style and language—what once the Master's closest pupils had learned from his own lips; facts they later had entrusted, in deeply symbolic language, to others who had come to them to seek their guidance.

While in its form the legend followed ancient models, it yet preserved the core of truth; for even though there were at that time seven Brothers who saw the public life of their new Brother from nearby, only three of them were in effect his teachers; and there must always be three Luminaries whenever a new link is to be added to the golden chain that, from the time that man appeared upon this planet, must be renewed in every generation.

The author of the ancient text, now called the "Gospel according to St. John," not only knew all this, but also wrote for others who were aware of many things they had been taught in secret.

Indeed, his text assumes the reader's knowledge of the Master's authentic teaching. To one who was instructed, this teaching brightly shone from many sayings in this text, while it remained well hidden from all who stood outside. For at that time the Spirit's law demanded such concealment.

But the Spirit too knows ebb and flow, knows ages of concealment and times of revelation. And thus one may today disclose what in the past demanded silence. Yet even so there is no danger that any uninvited guest might ever find the hidden temple where the Godhead dwells.

None will ever find the way to this eternal shrine but those who seek it from the purest fire of their heart: until they find the longed-for guidance—in themselves.

They shall indeed see mysteries reveal themselves before their eyes; and yet, however many wonders man will come to know through the millennia, far greater secrets shall forever wait for him at the horizon. In all eternity, however, the Godhead never will become accessible to mankind as an "object" that the intellect might comprehend.

Only parables and symbols can ever show the truth of ultimate Reality.

But one who seeks the Truth no more *without*, having grasped that man can only in his innermost behold it "face to face," he shall see that parables and symbols point the way into the inmost of Reality.

Much more can there be shown him still—if he be worthy. This, however, I here must leave unsaid, thus keeping it from all; be it that no human words are adequate to speak of it, or that such knowledge would be of no use unless one had it from within; for only here one truly *can* attain it.

༄

THE AFTERMATH

It is not up to me what I may say, for there are well-drawn limits that I must observe.

I may disclose no more than what I am permitted to convey, in order that the light again may penetrate the darkness.

There are in our time far more throughout the world who seek the light than there have been in any period of the past; and nowadays the written word indeed can safely reach them, without the former danger of corruption by being copied and transcribed.

Blest the hearts that hear my words and will be wrested from the darkness: that also they may find the Way—prepared by Love beyond all measure—and in themselves their "Resurrection."

CHAPTER FOUR

THE MISSIVE

NOT EVEN ONE WHO *HAS* THE FACULTY OF spiritual perception would be able to restore the very wording of the ancient Missive in its original form. What he may know through spiritual perception is, instead, the content and the aim of the authentic work; not, however, in the words of the historic tongue in which it first was written.

Perception in the realm of Spirit can only be attained in a condition of complete, indeed almost extreme, receptiveness of every sense and faculty. Thus it demands of one who still is subject to the laws of matter such extraordinary energies of concentration, if he would also *hold* before him what he wishes to discover, that the result would in the end not warrant the required effort, should one attempt to recreate the text of the entire Missive word for word. Only those who know the like perception from experience—and none but Luminaries living here as mortals acquire this experience—can also know what energies are used up during many years: before one learns to bring into the light of self-experience the thoughts that long ago a human being was seeking to express in words.

What in this way becomes one's own *experience* —not merely outward observation—must then again be rendered in one's proper words, so that the former author's aim and meaning be presented in a manner suited to a later age. However, one who thus can recreate an ancient source may also wish to use whatever fragments of the extant text he knows to be authentic.

Those for whom the text of Scripture is the very word of God may think all this a blasphemous abuse of Holy Writ; yet even others, who long discovered on their own how much of this disfigured text may be ascribed to "God," may well reject new readings of this work as pure imagination, if one were to declare that they are based on *spiritual* perception—without providing formal "proof."

∞

Even so, however, I shall have to include some fragments of the extant text, and I shall render them according to the author's meaning, which is manifest to spiritual perception.

But far be it from me to give offense to pious faith, which may grant comfort to an innocent believer and—if he be worthy—can even guide him to the Truth by ways most strange and roundabout.

Nor do I seek especially to recommend this book to formal scholars of the subject; even though I have good reasons for saying here that more than one old manuscript is likely yet to be discovered, which then will prove the accuracy of the text as I present it.*

To begin with, here is an example that will show how wantonly the zealots of the new religion were to change the ancient text after it had come into their hands.

In the original, the unknown author of the work had written words that meant the following:

---

*Twenty-three years after this was published the Dead Sea Scrolls were found at Qumrân; to date, however, no Johannine text has come to light.—Ed.

THE WISDOM OF ST. JOHN

IN THE BEGINNING IS THE WORD, AND THE WORD IS IN GOD, AND GOD IS THE WORD.

FROM IT ALONE HAS ALL THAT IS ITS BEING, AND THERE IS NOTHING THAT HAS BEING BUT FROM IT: NOT EVEN THE LEAST.

IT GIVES LIFE TO EVERYTHING THAT IS, AND ITS LIFE IS THE LIGHT OF MEN.

THE LIGHT SHINES IN THE DARKNESS, AND THE DARK CANNOT EXTINGUISH IT.

IT IS IN THE WORLD, AND THE WORLD HAS COME FROM IT, BUT THE WORLD KNOWS IT NOT.

IT IS WITHIN ITS OWN, YET THOSE WHO ARE ITS OWN DO NOT RECEIVE IT.

BUT ALL THAT DO RECEIVE IT, TO THEM IT GIVES THE POWER TO BECOME BEGOTTEN OUT OF GOD: NOT BEGOTTEN BY THE BLOOD, NEITHER BY THE WILL OF WOMAN, NOR BY THE WILL OF MAN, BUT OF GOD: OUT OF THE FULLNESS OF ALL GRACE AND TRUTH.

In the original, the context of this passage was not broken by interpolations; for the author here meant only to remind his pupils, to whom the Missive was addressed, of the way in which they were to read the text that followed. Therefore he began his prologue with these words, closely patterned on the doctrine of the "Logos," which then was widely known.

Only then did he begin to use the story of the Baptist, which he had found in older texts. However, he retold it in *his* way, because he sought to stress not only that he was in opposition to the pupils of the Baptist, who still existed at that time, but also meant to tell his readers that man's salvation is not found either by the strict asceticism practiced by the Baptist, himself a missionary of a mystic sect, nor by the baptism with water as propagated by the recent cult, which had assumed the Master's exalted name.

And then he also wanted to refute an older legend, which pretended that, before beginning his own ministry, the Master once had been a pupil of the Baptist.

This is why he shows the pupils leaving their former teacher when the latter must confess that *he* can only baptize men with water, whereas Jehoshuah could baptize them with Spirit.

Again according to their meaning, here are the author's words:

> THERE WAS A MAN WHO CALLED HIMSELF JEHOHANAN.
>
> AND THIS TOOK PLACE AT BETHANY BEYOND THE JORDAN, WHERE JEHOHANAN BAPTIZED.
>
> JEHOHANAN SAID: I BAPTIZE WITH WATER, BUT THERE IS ONE AMONG YOU, AND YOU DO NOT KNOW HIM: HE SHALL BAPTIZE WITH SPIRIT.
>
> I FEEL UNWORTHY TO LOOSEN EVEN THE LATCHET OF HIS SANDALS.
>
> BUT ON ANOTHER DAY JEHOHANAN STOOD THERE WITH TWO OF HIS DISCIPLES.
>
> AND WHEN HE SAW JEHOSHUAH WALK BY, HE SAID: THIS IS THE MAN.
>
> I KNEW HIM NOT MYSELF, BUT HE THAT SENT ME TO BAPTIZE WITH WATER SAID TO ME: IF YOU SHALL SEE A MAN ON WHOM A SPIRIT SHALL DESCEND, AND STAY IN HIM: HE IS THE ONE WHO SHALL COME TO BAPTIZE WITH SPIRIT.

AND JEHOHANAN BORE WITNESS, SAYING: I SAW A SPIRIT DESCENDING ON HIM FROM ABOVE, EVEN AS A DOVE ALIGHTS, AND THE SPIRIT REMAINED IN HIM.

AND WHEN THE TWO DISCIPLES HEARD HIM SAY THESE WORDS THEY FOLLOWED JEHOSHUAH.

If a translator nowadays had the original before him, he might express these sentences in different words; however, he could not arrive at a different meaning.

The author of the Missive was not at all concerned with having his account agree with those reports that later sought to use his text for proving that the Baptist had proclaimed the Master as the "Messiah."

Certain things are not included in the given passage, although they now form part of the accepted text. But all the words that would seem missing are subsequent interpolations, added by the very minds who had so altered the original that now the Baptist's name occurs already in the Missive's prologue.

In many ways the early writers sought to make their text agree with the three older records, which to them were Holy Writ.

What in the early phases of the new religion might be called a copy was little more than paraphrase, and every scribe who made one more such "copy" would think it quite in order so to change the text that it could serve to buttress *his* beliefs and doctrines.

And thus the Missive passed through many hands before it was to reach the form that stands at the beginning of the entire textual tradition.

To be sure, one may regret the loss of the original; but one should not—merely prompted by one's wishes—continue to defend the current text at any cost. Instead, one clearly ought to face the fact that most of it is changed and added, and that little still resembles the original.

Only those who have absorbed the teaching once conveyed by the Master to his closest pupils, and which was still alive among the few to whom the Missive was addressed—only those will know with certainty what still bears marks of the authentic text, and what is merely pious fraud.

Until one finds some ancient, well protected documents, or sources that at least are closer to the author's work than is the currently accepted text, this will remain the only way of gaining clarity in this regard.

© CHAPTER FIVE

THE AUTHENTIC TEACHING

The radiant master's profoundest teaching, which he entrusted only to his pupils, went far beyond the ethical instruction he gave in public to the people, and far beyond the sayings later taken from the "heathen" sages, and then ascribed to him.

This sublime teaching was not the issue of his intellect, nor had he found it in a state of pious ecstasy.

Everything he had to give to his few intimates, the pupils whom he meant to comprehend the "mystery of the kingdom of God," came from the eternal source of wisdom that is common to the spiritual Brotherhood of which he was a member. This ancient, sacred knowledge—which those who form this Brotherhood on earth find only in the light of highest self-awareness—he formulated in his way and in his language, as each who has this knowledge, by virtue of self-transformation, is but a witness to this selfsame Truth. Each will reveal it in his proper words and symbols, even though he may no less express it in the forms of old tradition.

Thus he knew to guide the pupils who could follow him into the very heart of Life eternal, and gave them a conception of the Godhead that differed greatly from the common doctrine of the priests.

HE SPOKE to men who had not studied in the schools, and who did understand him when he said of the Eternal Light, which "speaks" itself as the Eternal Word:

> GOD IS SPIRIT, AND THEY THAT WORSHIP HIM MUST WORSHIP TRUTH WITHIN THE SPIRIT.

But what he never tired of was telling his disciples of the *way* that leads into the kingdom of the Spirit, a kingdom that has "many mansions"—many forms of conscious life, each depending on the level of perception the human spirit can attain—once it has awakened.

It does not always mean the same when the Master speaks of the "kingdom of God."

To be sure, he says the kingdom of heaven is "in man"; but then he also says that none can "see" God's kingdom who is not first "reborn." Here one can avoid confusion only if one knows that in the one case he speaks merely of the human spirit's inborn possibilities, through which man can discover that the realm of Spirit does indeed exist, even though he lacks the faculties, while he is physically living, to be as fully conscious of himself within the Spirit's highest realms as he is physically conscious here on earth.

However, in the other case he speaks of the sublimest goal the human spirit has in the eternal: namely, that he shall attain—after this existence, and perhaps long preparation in the other life—a new and different reality of being, a form of life through which he then will be enabled to live and act within the Spirit's *inmost* realm.

֍

THAT IS to say, one must distinguish two successive forms of being. First of all, man must awaken from his sleep within the mortal creature. Arising from the night of his unknowing, man's spirit now begins to sense that his eternal home is not this earth, but that he came from realms of being where life is formed by laws quite unlike those he sees in the domain of physical perception.

This new awareness will then lead man to strive toward the Eternal Light, wherein, proceeding world by world through all the Spirit's hierarchies, man's spiritual self will ultimately find itself in everlasting life.

This striving toward Eternal Light may, however, reach fulfillment already in this present life, when a "scintilla" from the Spirit, a ray of the Eternal Light, descends through all the worlds and orders of the Spirit's life, and brings into existence within the human spirit, and from this spirit's proper substance, a *spiritual* organism that unites the human life with the divine "scintilla," that ray from the Eternal Light, which man will henceforth know as his eternal Living God.

What man may earlier have sensed but darkly, he now knows with full certainty: for he is conscious of his life within the Spirit, and knows that he is living by the Spirit's power.

But still he is by no means able to live and act as well within that lofty realm of Spirit from which he once had torn himself by his own will: in that "fall" from living Light that bound him to this world of physical perception.

Life in that highest realm needs something more; and even when man's spirit once has left this mortal form, to find itself alive and conscious in the lower spheres of spiritual existence, the very highest, inmost world of spiritual perception—the "kingdom of God" in the sublimest sense—will be forever closed to man until he is "reborn" into that world: begotten of the Spirit's seed, born of the living waters of eternal life within the Spirit.

"Birth" into the world of physical perception is the result of procreation by the mortal creature, and only birth creates the possibility for man to consciously exist and act within the physical dimension.

Unless a man is "born" into this world he cannot enter it by any other way; it is forever closed to him, even if he knew that it existed.

And likewise, no one can ever enter any of the worlds of spiritual perception—and everything within the Spirit is to itself *perception*—except he first were *born* in them.

In the beginning, the human spirit was, however, "born" into that inmost "realm of God," God-begotten from eternity, but when he left this realm, he also left behind, to use this image, his spiritual, God-born organism, which then resolved itself again into the elements of Godhead; and thus an individual "rebirth" must occur before the human spirit will be able consciously to live and act within that inmost "realm of God."

Before this has occurred, the human spirit—even at the highest level of perfection it may achieve through life on earth—is only conscious of itself and of its Living God; thus, following the "death" of its material body, it only finds itself within the Spirit's lower spheres, whose organism it retained in rudimental form despite its "fall" into the world of physical perception. This rudimental organism is the only form of spiritual life the human being still possesses, and which it can develop by its conduct in this present life.

It is, however, only of man's last and highest goal that the author of the Missive lets the Master say:

> UNLESS A MAN BE BORN AGAIN OUT OF THE WATERS OF THE SPIRIT—AND OF THE SPIRIT'S SEED—HE CANNOT ENTER THE KINGDOM OF GOD.

And for the sake of emphasis and clarity, he has the Master add:

> THAT WHICH IS BORN OF THE FLESH IS FLESH, AND THAT WHICH IS BORN OF THE SPIRIT IS SPIRIT . . .

lest there be the slightest doubt that here he speaks about the generation of a real organism: as of the flesh, so also of the Spirit.

The only beings on this earth, however, who do attain this "rebirth" in the Spirit already in their mortal life, and thus are consciously alive and active within the Spirit's inmost realm, yet also have their faculties for physical perception, are the Luminaries, the Bearers of

Eternal Light. And one of these was in his day the radiant Master of Nazareth.

Only one who is a Luminary can in truth declare, both of himself and of his Brothers:

> WE SPEAK OF WHAT WE KNOW, AND WE BEAR WITNESS TO THAT WHICH WE HAVE SEEN.

Or again that other word, which later was inserted in an added episode, where now it scarcely can be recognized:

> YOU WORSHIP WHAT YOU DO NOT KNOW, BUT WE KNOW WHAT WE WORSHIP.

❧

But like the great Master himself, so every Luminary must profess:

> I AND THE FATHER ARE ONE. HE THAT SEES ME ALSO SEES THE FATHER.

Because the "Father," who is in the Eternal Word, has no other self-representation on this earth except the Luminary, the Bearer of Eternal Light; one whom the Father himself brought forth to be his self-representation, and for whom he has created, of himself, the spiritual organism that gives the Luminary conscious life within the worlds of spiritual perception, without removing him from physical existence.

The Luminary thus has in the true sense of the word become a "Son" of the "Father" in the Eternal Word, a Son who has been born into the present world.

THE AUTHENTIC teaching the Master revealed is based upon his conscious knowledge of being the spiritual Son of the eternal spiritual Father, and on his self-experience within the worlds of spiritual perception.

> YES, YOU KNOW ME, AND ALSO KNOW WHERE I AM FROM. BUT I CAME NOT ON MY OWN—NOT MY EARTHLY PARENTAGE GAVE ME THE RIGHT TO TEACH AND SPEAK TO YOU AS I AM SPEAKING —BUT I AM SENT BY ONE WHO IS THE TRUTH, AND HIM YOU DO NOT KNOW.

> THOUGH I BEAR WITNESS OF MYSELF, MY WITNESS IS THE TRUTH; FOR I KNOW WHERE I CAME FROM AND WHERETO I SHALL GO.

TRULY, HE THAT SENT ME IS WITH ME, AND HE DOES NOT FORSAKE ME; BECAUSE I ALWAYS DO WHAT PLEASES HIM.

And from the fullest knowledge that in the world around him only he alone knew what is needed if mortal man—"at the last day" in this present life—is to find himself prepared for his eternal birth into the world of spiritual perception, the Master spoke the mighty words:

I AM THE WAY, THE TRUTH, AND THE LIFE; NO MAN COMES TO THE FATHER EXCEPT THROUGH ME.

For the Spirit-born identity that, as a Luminary, he experiences as his proper self, and which he calls the "Son," remains the same reality for every human spirit; and only in this Son can any human spirit ever find eternal life within the world of Spirit.

It is that very life of which he has experience, and of that life he therefore can bear witness:

WHAT MY FATHER HAS GIVEN ME IS GREATER THAN ALL THINGS, AND NO ONE CAN PLUCK IT FROM MY FATHER'S HAND.

But it is not for himself alone that he would have eternal life, and so he says:

> HE THAT BELIEVES IN ME BELIEVES NOT ME, BUT HIM THAT SENT ME.
>
> I CAME INTO THE WORLD TO BE A LIGHT: THAT NO ONE WHO BELIEVES IN ME SHOULD LIVE IN DARKNESS.
>
> FOR I HAVE NOT SPOKEN ON MY OWN; BUT THE FATHER WHO SENT ME, HE GAVE ME THE COMMANDMENT WHAT I AM TO SPEAK AND TEACH.
>
> AND I KNOW THAT HIS COMMANDMENT COMES FROM LIFE ETERNAL.
>
> THEREFORE, WHAT I SAY I SAY EVEN AS THE FATHER HAS TOLD ME.

The Luminary, the Bearer of Eternal Light, is the vessel through which the Father in the Son reveals himself on earth in temporal *self-representation*. The Luminary, however, knows himself as Son of the eternal Father—the highest spiritual sovereign of all the Luminaries here on earth—in whom all members of that timeless Brotherhood live unified as one identity. And likewise, it is only through the Luminary that the Father—Aeonic Man, born in the Eternal Word, in the Beginning—is known on earth in mortal human revelation.

> EVEN AS THE FATHER HAS LIFE OF HIMSELF, SO ALSO HAS HE GIVEN TO THE SON TO HAVE LIFE OF HIMSELF.

However, in the same way that Moses in the wilderness had raised the serpent of bronze, so that all who looked on it with faith might live, so also must the image of the "Son of Man," the Luminary, be raised above all else in mortal man: in the faith and knowledge of the truth that the Eternal Light reveals itself in the Eternal Word; which "speaks" itself as the Eternal Man of the Beginning, who in his light-begotten glory abides forever in the Word, and becomes the "Father" to the Luminaries, so that the human spirit on this earth—through them—might hear again of its eternal home and origin, and of the way that leads it back.

> EVEN AS MOSES LIFTED UP THE SERPENT IN THE WILDERNESS, SO ALSO MUST THE SON OF MAN—THE WITNESS FROM THE KINGDOM OF THE SPIRIT, AND HIS MESSAGE—BE RAISED: THAT NO ONE WHO BELIEVES IN HIM MAY PERISH—IN

AEONS OF NIGHT AND UNKNOWING—
BUT HAVE LIFE.

AND AGAIN, to show that only he finds proof who trusts the Luminaries in the way that those who wanted to recover had to trust in Moses' wondrous serpent, the author of the Missive has the Master say:

> WHEN YOU HAVE LIFTED UP THE SON OF MAN, THEN YOU WILL KNOW THAT I AM HE, AND THAT I WORK NOTHING ON MY OWN—AS MORTAL MAN ACCORDING TO MY HUMAN WILL—BUT ONLY SPEAK WHAT MY FATHER HAS TAUGHT ME.

AGAIN AND again he emphasizes that the Luminary, the Bearer of Eternal Light, who manifests the highest form of spiritual perception attainable to man on earth, one who knows to unify the sublimest life within the Spirit with the mortal human creature, never teaches from his merely human wisdom, but from the fullness of all knowledge that the Father has revealed to him.

MY TEACHING IS NOT MINE, BUT HIS THAT SENT ME. IF ANY MAN WILL DO HIS WILL, HE SHALL DISCOVER WHETHER THIS TEACHING IS FROM GOD, OR WHETHER IT IS FROM ME.

Thus he states that the condition on which all proof as to the Luminary's teaching rests is twofold; in that the pupil first must grasp the meaning of the awesome fact that a mortal human being can bring authentic knowledge from the inmost realm of Spirit; and second, that now he also will conduct himself according to the Spirit's laws, which the Luminary—*one* with the Father, and obedient to the Father's will—has come to make known in this world.

But the Luminary's work is not restricted to the world of physical perception.

Instead, his powers do extend from the inmost realm of Spirit—the sphere of final causes—to the world of matter, but also to the Spirit's lower spheres: the regions that the human spirit enters when he leaves this present life. Concerning this the Master says:

THE HOUR IS COMING, AND ALREADY IT HAS COME: WHEN THE DEAD —THROUGH ME—SHALL HEAR THE VOICE OF THE SON; AND THEY THAT HEAR IT SHALL LIVE—FOR SUCH THE LUMINARY CAN AWAKEN AND PREPARE FOR THEIR REBIRTH IN THE SPIRIT BY THE FATHER.

But that no one might assume that he—even as the Son of the Father—ever acted on his own, he has this to say:

THE SON CAN OF HIMSELF WORK NOTHING, EXCEPT HE SEE THE FATHER DO IT; FOR EVERYTHING THE FATHER DOES, THAT WILL THE SON DO LIKEWISE.

NO ONE CAN COME TO ME UNLESS THE FATHER WHO HAS SENT ME DRAW HIM TO ME: THAT I AWAKEN HIM AT HIS LAST DAY.

No HUMAN spirit can find eternal life within the Spirit's world, however, unless it have the *faith* that it indeed *will* find this life.

And only of *this* kind of faith, which must be trust in *one's own self*, the Master once had spoken in connection with his teaching: a teaching that brought final certainty out of the world of Spirit, and brought it through the mouth of man.

> THIS IS THE BREAD WHICH CAME FROM HEAVEN, THAT NO ONE WHO SHALL EAT OF IT MAY PERISH.

These words appeared originally in the same place where he said:

> HE THAT BELIEVES IN ME: RIVERS OF LIVING WATER SHALL FLOW FROM HIS BODY—

for he shall then, out of himself, continue to give life to things within the world of spiritual perception; for here the Master speaks about the "body" of one who has been *reborn* in the Spirit.

He also meant *this* body, the organism of one who has been reborn in the Spirit, when he said in this connection that, in the world of spiritual perception, this body is in every way as real as *flesh* and *blood* are *real* in the world of matter; so that no one could have conscious life in the dimensions of the Spirit except he were endowed with such a body.

THE AUTHENTIC TEACHING

UNLESS YOU COME TO HAVE THE FLESH OF THE SON OF MAN, AND HIS BLOOD BE IN YOU, YOU WILL NOT IN YOURSELVES HAVE LIFE.

A<small>LL THAT</small> now is found in the traditional version of the Missive, in the passage where the words about the "bread from heaven" are mingled with the sayings regarding "flesh" and "blood," is the work of later editors, and purposeful interpolation.

What he had said about the spiritual body appeared well suited to support the recent cult, which had developed from the rites and customs of the mystery religions that could be found throughout the Orient at that time.

And thus the Master's words were changed in such a way that he appeared to be referring to his *mortal* flesh and blood, and not to the reality that, in the inmost kingdom of the Spirit, bore his *spiritual* consciousness, as here on earth his physical and human consciousness was borne by *mortal* flesh and blood.

Those who edited the Missive would write their own opinions into any paraphrases of this text, and at the same time linked it closely with his words about the "bread from heaven."

※

To be sure, among the men who later formed the new religion's cult and liturgy there was more than one who had indeed found light and knowledge; however, they were compelled to deal with creeds that were by then established, and could do little but correct through their interpretation what they found incorporated from some alien cults.

But some of these who knew were in the end expelled as "heretics;" while the interpretations of some others were accepted only insofar as this seemed possible without thereby endangering the doctrines that were taken from old pagan cults, because to these the new religion owed its mystic nimbus.

It is, however, anything but accidental that this Missive—even in its currently accepted, edited condition—is the only Gospel that has not a word to say about the Master's declarations on the feast of the Last Supper—the very words on which the older records had based and founded the new cult.

Surely one would think that—of any author—the writer of the Missive, into whose text one had inserted the fictitious words about the Master's earthly flesh and blood: "For my flesh is meat indeed, and my blood is drink indeed," would have recorded with most solemn emphasis those of all words spoken at the Last Supper! If, that is, there ever had been any record of a single word of even remotely similar meaning that the Master might have said on the occasion that the earlier texts had forged.

But as it was, the author of the Missive knew full well that these pronouncements were concepts from old pagan cults, which now had found a new direction based upon the Master's name.

THIS WAS the very point, however, that altogether separated the *spiritual* knowledge by which the author's life was guided, and which he sought to strengthen also in his pupils, from the doctrine and the outward cult that had begun to grow around the Master's name. At the time he wrote his text, this cult had already achieved a measure of success, because its missionaries sought in every way to fit the Master's sayings to the various communities and doctrines of the mystery religions that they encountered everywhere.

∽

INDEED, TO understand this Missive fully one has to know that its author wrote it to point out the *difference* between the Master's profoundest teaching, which few have grasped in any age, and the emerging creeds and speculations of the outward cult, which more and more began to yoke the minds, and owed its progress in no small degree to the way in which it integrated the new and the traditional, so that every mystic doctrine of the age could therein find new meaning.

But since the outward cult had also mingled with its speculations many sayings of the Master that were sacred to John's followers as well, the author sought to guard the wavering among his little circle, and to save them from the present danger of succumbing to the public cult.

But in the end the Missive was unable to achieve the purpose for which the author had composed it.

The last descendants of John's pupils were forced to yield before the public cult; its followers saw them as "heretics," and so they had to live in hiding. Thus, not quite a generation later there was none left who still lived in the knowledge of the Master's authentic teaching.

And when the Missive later fell into the hands of pious zealots of the new religion, scribe after scribe found cause to write into this text, which they could in good faith consider as the work of the apostle John, anything that made it useful for public readings in their meetings.

The reverential awe in face of Holy Writ did not have, for the nascent Faith, the great significance it was to gain in later ages.

Far more important then was still the cultus of the new Redeemer-God, and the defense of speculations and beliefs against both Jews and heathen.

And so the texts were altered without hesitation to satisfy the cult's demands, which now sought also to interpret the rites of ancient mysteries. Nor had converted Jews and Gentiles, who composed the congregations, any scruples when it came to altering a text they felt might prove an obstacle when dealing with their former coreligionists.

All were convinced that in so doing they only served the propagation of the "true" belief, and thus were ultimately acting fully in the spirit of the former authors.

It is almost a miracle that, all this notwithstanding, scattered parts of the authentic text have yet survived; even though the sense of many sayings was so altered that today they mean the opposite.

But one who will search deeper, and clears away the layers of debris, can even now discover in this work the fundaments beneath an ancient temple, whose shrine preserved the undistorted teaching that the Master of Nazareth, as a Bearer of Eternal Light, had once entrusted to his closest pupils.

CHAPTER SIX

THE PARACLETE

The radiant master who in his life on earth became the Lord of Love knew well indeed that the sublimest work of love, which he one day was to accomplish, could only be accomplished in the hour of his death, and only in a death that he would suffer at the hand of man.

Thus, he knew times when he desired that his death were near, and other times, when thoughts about his end filled him with horror. One day he could long to see his final hour, another day he hoped the end were far away, so that he might be longer near his pupils: to give them later what as yet "they could not bear."

At such times of fear and horror he would go to see his venerated Brothers in their desert solitude; but they could only tell him that one who has become the Father's Son in the Eternal Light must never seek to know the things that are to be.

Once, however, when his soul was troubled by such thoughts and he sensed that the end was near, but without knowing when the time would be, the Master wrote a letter for his pupils from this desert solitude and sent it to the one he "loved"; for John could understand him more deeply than the others, because the love they felt for one another had opened that pupil's soul.

M<small>ANY WORDS</small> and sayings that the Missive's author gives as *spoken* are in fact quotations from such letters written by the Master's hand. In the present case, however, the text of almost the entire letter has survived, even though it later was fragmented and used in other contexts: where it better served the dogmas of the nascent cult.

In the original Missive, the author had preserved the letter from the Master's hand as follows:

> YET A LITTLE WHILE, AND THE WORLD WILL NO LONGER SEE ME.

THE PARACLETE

ON THAT DAY YOU CANNOT ASK ME ANY MORE QUESTIONS.

HOWEVER, I SHALL NOT ABANDON YOU AS ORPHANS.

I SHALL ASK THE FATHER, AND HE WILL SEND YOU ANOTHER GUIDE FROM THE SPIRIT OF TRUTH: ONE WHOM THE WORLD CANNOT SEIZE, BECAUSE IT NEITHER SEES HIM, NOR KNOWS OF HIM.

BUT YOU SHALL KNOW HIM, FOR HE WILL STAY WITH YOU, AND SHALL BE IN YOU.

HE WILL TEACH AND RECALL TO YOU ALL THE THINGS THAT I HAVE TOLD YOU.

HE SHALL NOT SPEAK ON HIS AUTHORITY—EVEN AS I TOLD YOU THAT I SPEAK NOT ON MY OWN AUTHORITY—BUT THAT WHICH HE HEARS HE WILL SPEAK AND MAKE IT KNOWN TO YOU.

HE SHALL BE A WITNESS UNTO ME: FOR HE SHALL TAKE FROM WHAT IS MINE TO MAKE IT KNOWN TO YOU.

EVERYTHING THE FATHER HAS IS MINE. THEREFORE I SAY: HE SHALL TAKE FROM WHAT IS MINE.

HE THAT RECEIVES THE ONE THAT I SHALL SEND RECEIVES ME; AND HE THAT RECEIVES ME RECEIVES THE ONE THAT SENT ME.

ON THAT DAY YOU SHALL KNOW THAT I AM IN MY FATHER.

LET NOT YOUR HEART BE TROUBLED.

BE WITHOUT FEAR.

I LEAVE YOU BEHIND IN PEACE.

I GIVE YOU MY PEACE, WHICH THE WORLD CANNOT GIVE.

THE MEANING of this letter is, thus, nothing other than the Master's promise to his pupils that he would send another teacher to instruct them when he himself should be no longer with them. He says, however, that this teacher would be one among those Luminaries who live no more in mortal, but in their spiritual form, so that they might attain their highest goal through him, without the fear that men might seize and tear him from their midst, as they had done with him.

He clearly stresses in this letter that, like himself, the coming teacher from the Spirit, whom they only could hear in themselves, would also not be speaking on his own authority, and that he too would only teach them what they once had heard from him.

And like every Son of the eternal Father, also the promised teacher would be taking from the timeless wisdom of the Father, and thus he would confirm what he himself had taught.

But since the Master's person had soon become a "God" to the believers of the new religion, it was natural that also the Master's spiritual Brother would very soon be deified.

One had failed to comprehend the ultimate Tri-Unity, which in truth is only this: Eternal Light—unformed and all-embracing: the infinite, incomprehensible, and everlasting "Sea of Godhead"—reveals itself as One in the Eternal Word which is in the "Beginning" that ever was, and is, and shall be: "God" within the Godhead. And the Eternal Word in turn reveals, out of itself, Eternal Man: the Light-begotten, everlasting, highest Being in the

Spirit, who is forever in the Word and, as the Father, manifests Himself through all the Spirit's living hierarchies.

Thus, while being One, the Father is at once the root and source of All and all infinity: revealing Himself to Himself in the numbers of the Origin, from which proceed infinities upon infinities of lives within the Spirit's universe.

※

THIS ULTIMATE reality of spiritual life is, thus, at once the Spirit's own self-revelation and, equally, this revelation's spiritual result:

> the All Incomprehensible,
> the All in One,
> the One in All,

which in turn will manifest itself in Oneness without end. This in truth is ultimate reality, whatever words are used to represent it; for one indeed might also call it:

> Life Eternal: Unrevealed,
> Life Eternal: Self-Revealing,
> Life Eternal: Revealed.

But human language has no words that might convey more than a vague reflection of the

Spirit's life, whose full reality is only comprehended through the faculty of love. And even now it is this faculty through which the human spirit once again is able to regain its erstwhile life in God, from which it long ago had torn itself by its own will.

The "Spirit of Truth" is in reality, however, the very life of the Eternal Word: it is Eternal Light itself, incomprehensible and infinite, which manifests itself as the Eternal Word. Within this Word the Spirit's countless hierarchies have life and being, which may be likened to the tone and voice of the Eternal Word: the Word's eternally proceeding revelation in the spiritual cosmos of Eternal Light.

Even the lower form of spiritual life that man retained despite his "fall" from highest Light has its existence only from this selfsame "Spirit of Truth," which is the spiritual substance of Eternal Light. And from this Light the human spirit can receive within itself, already in this present life, a spiritual *scintilla*, which man will know from then on as his Living God.

THE WISDOM OF ST. JOHN

Eternal Light remains the final source of life in everything that lives: it is the life that is *in being through itself.*

Incomprehensible within itself as being, it "speaks" itself in the Eternal Word, which thus is likewise given: *being through itself.*

And proceeding in its generations, the Word in turn reveals itself in the Eternal Human of the Spirit, who also is *in being through Himself* only through Eternal Light, and thus continues to bring forth, out of Himself, the countless hierarchies of beings in the Spirit, all of which again have *being through themselves*, since all in truth are merely revelations—more or less removed from the Eternal Light—that are made manifest by the Eternal Word, which is itself the first eternal revelation of that Light.

The one and all-embracing impulse in all these revelations of eternal life, however, is the Love that loves *itself* within *another*.

One who means to find his way into the Spirit, and in himself would know the life of the

Eternal Light anew: let him seek first and foremost always to "abide in love."

For him one shall unlock the "strait gate" that leads into eternal life; for he has learned to "knock": he seeks the way one ought to seek, and him will surely find—the Paraclete.

CONCLUSION

Wherever in this book I have included excerpts from the now accepted text, I did this only when I could be certain that they still convey the meaning of the lost original; where this was not the case, I used my own words to restore this meaning.

Since here I only deal with the interpretation of the Missive that tradition holds to be the "Gospel according to St. John," I knowingly have left aside the earlier three records of the Master's life, despite the fact that many words I know to be authentic in these texts would have confirmed my explanations.

But any reader who can follow my account will soon be able to discover for himself what is authentic in those older works; nor will he find it difficult to understand the reasons that are behind the changes and insertions in each case, not only in the Missive, but also in those older sources.

To be sure, one must concede that many words at one time much revered by people brought up to believe that Scripture is the work of God, words that may be sacred to them even now, are in truth poetic fictions of a later age.

But if such words in any way embody truth, I see no reason why they now should be less highly thought of, or rejected.

Those who later edited the ancient texts—if they be judged as *poets*—were often far superior to the original authors. For in their efforts to inform the extant sources with the dogma they were serving, they found both many symbols and new forms for older legends that might have been the envy of the earlier authors.

However, it is one thing to establish the authentic content of the Missive, and another to seek edifying inspiration in the witness of a poet who was writing to create a document for the belief he fervently embraced.

CONCLUSION

But since the ancient text considered in the present book had long been overlaid with poetry, so that the only source was falsified through which the Master's genuine teaching, which he had given only to his closest pupils, might have been transmitted to posterity, it was essential to restore the uncorrupted substance of the author's work—whenever any text had to be cited.

Owing to a form of diction that let each phrase stand by itself, and nearly gave it independent meaning—even taken out of proper context—every persuasion found it easy during the initial period to omit or add material at discretion, and so to make the text most useful for the cause.

And if the writers came upon a word they did not like, they would not scruple to eliminate authentic parts of the original, calling them "heretical" interpolations. And words that seemed too weighty to be left out altogether would be given some addition that completely changed their meaning.

It was another favorite device to take some word once spoken by the Master in a wholly different context, and then to use it in connection with one of the new wonder-legends that had begun appearing soon after his death; for in this way the writers sought to lend more credence to these tales.

Many words were thus eliminated, many others changed to mean the opposite—and still the traces of the Master's genuine teaching have survived. And to this day the timeless love shines through the pages of this ancient text: the love—the heritage of the apostle—that lived on even in the last of his successors. The author of the Missive too was one who knew this love, the light of the authentic teaching, which he sought to preserve for his disciples: pure as he himself had once received it; free from all dogmatic speculations, whose errors he saw all too clearly.

As for the other texts that, like this Missive, were ascribed to the disciple whom the Master "loved"—because he saw that love inspired him—it should be pointed out that none are from this pupil's hand, nor were they written by the author of the Missive.

CONCLUSION

The texts one is accustomed to regard as the "Epistles of John" surely do contain inspired words and enlightened wisdom of one whose spirit did "abide in love," but these epistles were not written until the Missive here discussed already had been edited to serve the new religion, and their author wrote as a believer of that faith.

The Apocalypse, however—the so-called Book of Revelation—is the work of many and unequal minds: a document from various periods.

In it one finds the traces of authentic knowledge, side by side with the hermetic glitter added by the faithful of the new religion, and finally the generous expansions supplied by later editors.

The one who finally endowed this book with the poetic grandeur of its diction had merely brought together already extant fragments of older mystical visions.

The Master's authentic teaching, which he had once revealed to no one but his closest pupils, and which only one of them, the one he "loved," had fully understood—who then disclosed it to his own disciples—this teaching is today found only in this Missive: the work of one who lived in later times, enlightened by the Spirit of that teaching.

M<small>AY THEN</small> the timeless wisdom that to this day shines brightly through this text — despite the fate it had to suffer—may this wisdom not be lost to those who shall seek knowledge in the days to come.

REMINDER

"Yet here I must point out again that if one would derive the fullest benefit from studying the books I wrote to show the way into the Spirit, one has to read them in the original; even if this should require learning German.

"Translations can at best provide assistance in helping readers gradually perceive, even through the spirit of a different language, what I convey with the resources of my mother tongue."

From "Answers to Everyone" (1933), *Gleanings*. Bern: Kobersche Verlagsbuchhandlung, 1990

Closely related to the
subject of the present book are
the following works by Bô Yin Râ:

The Book on Love
The Mystery of Golgotha
Resurrection
Life's Highest Goal

www.ingramcontent.com/pod-product-compliance
Lightning Source LLC
Chambersburg PA
CBHW022153080426
42734CB00006B/411